# Living Things

### Terry Jennings
Illustrated by **David Anstey**

## CONTENTS

SMITHMARK

# THE LIVING WORLD

**There are more than a million kinds of animals and almost 350,000 different kinds of plants. The largest animal that has ever lived is the blue whale. The largest plant in the world is a giant sequoia tree.**

The smallest animals and plants are so tiny that you could get hundreds of them on one of the periods on this page. They are all living things. What does it mean to be alive?

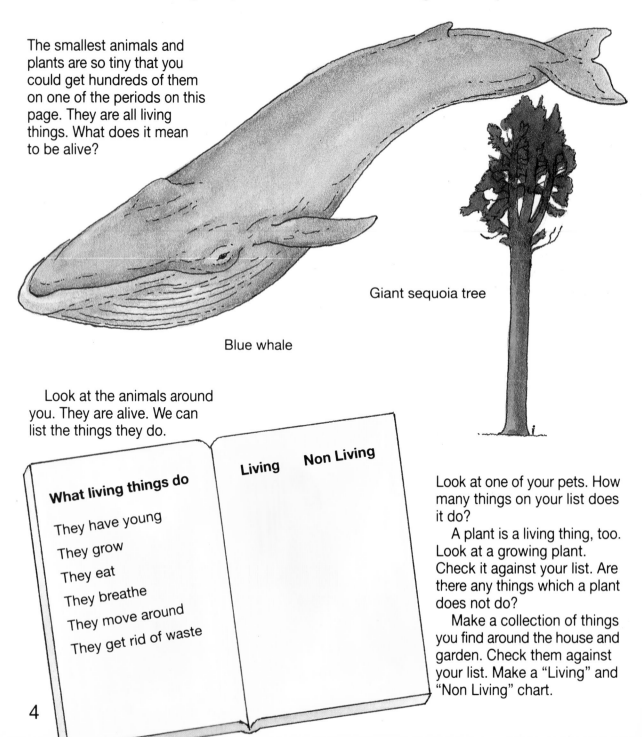

Giant sequoia tree

Blue whale

Look at the animals around you. They are alive. We can list the things they do.

**What living things do**

They have young

They grow

They eat

They breathe

They move around

They get rid of waste

Living    Non Living

Look at one of your pets. How many things on your list does it do?

A plant is a living thing, too. Look at a growing plant. Check it against your list. Are there any things which a plant does not do?

Make a collection of things you find around the house and garden. Check them against your list. Make a "Living" and "Non Living" chart.

# WHAT IS A WEED?

*Weeds* are plants. Without plants there would be no animals and humans would not exist. See page 26.

**1** Dig up a dandelion plant and shake off the soil.

**2** Lay it on some sheets of newspaper and look at the various parts carefully. How many of the parts shown in the picture can you see?

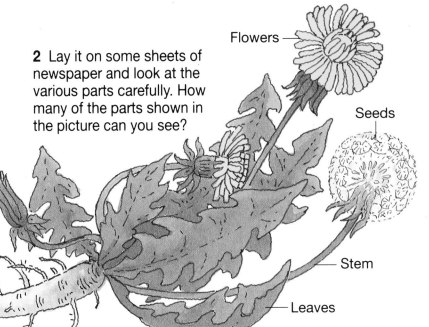

Flowers

Seeds

Stem

Leaves

Roots

# A PLANT LIFE CYCLE

All living things have a *life cycle*. This is a series of stages the plant or animal goes through as it grows up.

Search around the garden for a small weed. Carefully dig it up.

**1** Put it in a pot of topsoil or potting soil on a windowsill.

**2** Water it to keep the soil moist, but not too wet.

Measure your plant every week. How much does it grow?

**3** Does your weed produce flowers? What are these like?

What do the flowers turn into? If these things are put on the moist soil in another pot, will they grow? What eventually happens to your plant?

Look at some other garden plants. Do they all have the same parts?

Groundsel

Shepherd's purse

# FLOWER POWER

**We have seen how garden weeds produce flowers. Do all plants have flowers? Look around your garden or local park. Do grasses have flowers? Are all flowers brightly colored?**

## LOOKING AT FLOWERS

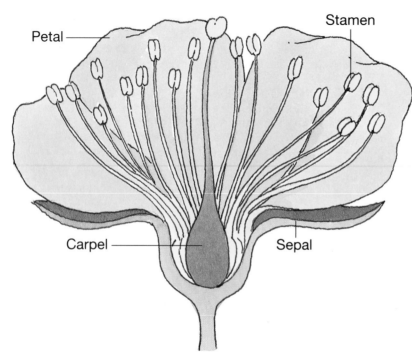

**1** Collect one or two large garden flowers. Take them apart. Look at them with a magnifying glass.

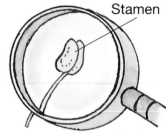

**2** Compare your flowers with the one in the picture. Do they have the same parts? Can you see the yellow dusty substance called *pollen* on the *stamens*? Can you see the *carpels* and *sepals*? Do your flowers have a sweet smell? This is to attract insects to them.

## INSECTS AND FLOWERS

On a warm sunny day sit quietly near some garden plants and watch the insects visit the flowers. Make a chart like this.

| Color of flower | Name of insect |
|---|---|
| Yellow | |
| Red | |

Before you leave, count up and see which color flower each kind of insect likes best. Why do insects go to flowers?

# PAPER FLOWERS

Will insects visit a paper flower? You can find out in this next experiment.

**You will need:** colored tissue paper; lollipop stick; tape; sugar; water.

**1** Cut out the shape of your flower and wrap it carefully around the stick.

**2** Secure your flower with tape.

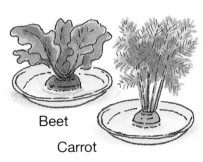

**3** Stir some sugar in a little water and paint it on the middle of your flower. Place the paper flower among real flowers and plants.

**4** Make a chart of how many insects and what types of insects visit your flower.

# NEW PLANTS FROM OLD

We can grow new plants from seeds. We can also grow new plants from pieces of plants.

**1** Cut off the top of a pineapple. Put it into a pot of moist potting soil.

**2** Put the pot inside a plastic bag and stand it on a warm, sunny windowsill.

Look carefully every day to see what is happening to your new plant.

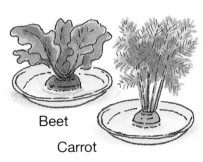

Beet

Carrot

**3** Break leafy shoots off mint plants, willow trees, or privet hedges. Stand them in bottles of water. Do they grow roots? If they do, plant your rooted *cuttings*, as they are called, in the garden or in pots of moist topsoil or potting soil.

Try growing cuttings and pieces of other plants in bottles or saucers of water.

Mint

Willow

# BULBS AND BEANS

There are lots more ways of making new plants. One of the easiest is to grow *bulbs*. Bulbs are really large buds. Around them is a layer of leaves containing food. An onion is a bulb. You can see the bud and the leaves containing food if you carefully cut an onion in half.

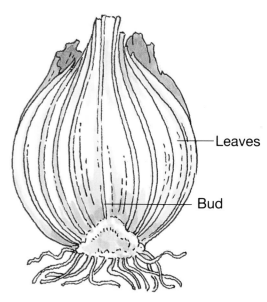

Leaves

Bud

## GROWING BULBS IN WATER

Most bulbs have to be planted in pots of potting soil, or out in the garden. Onions and some flower bulbs such as hyacinths will grow in water alone. Why don't you grow one?

**You will need:** a bulb; jar; small yogurt container; water.

Make sure your yogurt container fits neatly in the top of your jar.

**1** Ask an adult to cut out the bottom of the container. Push it into the top of the jar and fill the jar with water.

Yogurt container

**2** Stand a large bulb (or an onion) in the container.

**3** Put it in a dark place until the roots are about 4 inches (10 cm) long. Then bring it out onto a sunny windowsill.

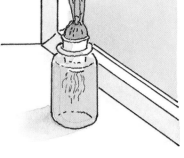

**4** Watch the new plant grow. What happens to the bulb as the new plant grows?

## BLOTTING-PAPER SEEDS

Here is a different way of growing seeds.

**1** Line a jar with blotting paper. Pour in an inch of water. Watch it slowly creep up the blotting paper.

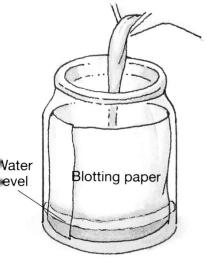

Water level
Blotting paper

**2** Slip two or three pea or bean seeds between the glass and the blotting paper.

**3** Watch the seeds grow. Draw them. What happens if you sow some of the seeds upside down or sideways? Try it and see.

## INSIDE A BEAN

**1** Soak a fava bean or string bean seed in cold water overnight. The next day split the seed open.

**2** Look at the inside of the seed with a magnifying glass. Can you see a tiny plant? It is called an *embryo*. The embryo uses the food stored inside the seed to grow into a new plant.

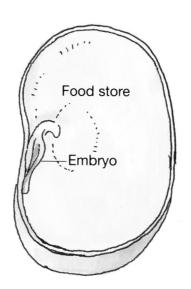

Food store

Embryo

### Bottle Trees

Some large fruits and seeds will also grow in water.

1  Find some bottles with narrow necks. Fill them with water. Stand an acorn or horse chestnut on top of each bottle.

2  Stand the bottles on a sunny windowsill. Remember that some tree fruits and seeds are very slow to grow.

Which grows first, the root or the shoot?

# FUN WITH SEEDS

**As we have seen, most plants can be grown from seeds. We can buy the seeds in packs. Most of these seeds are very small. Have you ever wondered why the seeds do not grow in the pack? The project on the next page will help you to understand why.**

## YOUR VERY OWN BEAN STALK

Have you read the story about "Jack and the Beanstalk"? It is quite easy to grow your own beanstalk.

**You will need:** a large flower pot with topsoil or potting soil; string bean seed; water.

**1** Push your seed into the soil so that it is just below the surface.

**2** Put the pot on a sunny windowsill and water it. Do not let the soil in the pot dry out. Check it daily.

**3** When the plant begins to bend over, tie it to a stick in the soil.

**4** You can keep a growth chart. Write down the dates that the shoot, leaves, and flowers first show. Measure the shoot every week until the leaves appear.

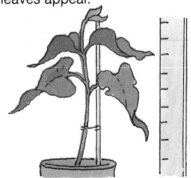

Does your runner bean plant grow bean pods? What is inside them? How many new plants could you grow from them?

# HAIRY EGG MEN

**You will need:** 4 clean egg shells; modeling clay; cotton; colored pens or paints; alfalfa seeds; water.

**1** Make four cups out of your modeling clay. Rest an egg shell in each cup, and paint a face on each one.

**2** Fill each egg man with cotton and sprinkle alfalfa seeds on top.

**3** Give each egg man a number from 1 to 4 and make a chart like this.

| Egg man | Hair growth | Hair color |
|---|---|---|
| 1 Wet and sunny | | |
| 2 Dry and sunny | | |
| 3 Wet and dark | | |
| 4 Under water | | |

**4** Wet the cotton of egg men 1 and 3. Put egg man 1 on a sunny windowsill and egg man 3 in a dark cool closet. Don't let the cotton dry out.

**5** Keep egg man 2 dry, but put him on a sunny windowsill.

2

**6** Put egg man 4 in a jar and cover him with water.

4

**7** Record on your chart which of the egg men grow hair and which do not. Why is this? Is the hair always the same color?

# SEEDS FAR AND WIDE

**Seeds have to be scattered. Otherwise they will all grow in one place and the young plants will be very weak. Many plants have special ways of scattering their seeds. Some, such as the lupin, explode shooting their seeds away from the parent plant. Others, such as the coconut, float away to a new place.**

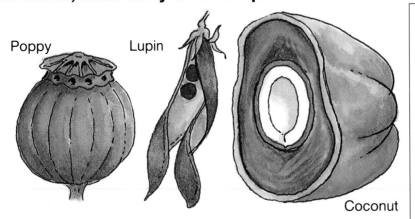

Poppy      Lupin

Coconut

## Winged Seeds

Some tree seeds have wings. They can whirl away from the tree like little helicopters. Sycamore and maple seeds do this.

**1** In the fall, take one and throw it up in the air. Watch the seed whirl down to the ground.

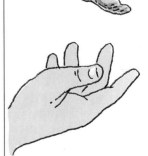

**2** Cut the wing off a maple or sycamore seed. Will it still whirl around? If you plant the seed, will it still grow?

## SEEDS SCATTERED BY WIND

Some seeds are scattered by the wind.

**1** Blow gently on a dandelion "puff." Watch the seeds float away.

**2** Blow away just one of the seeds and measure how far it travels. What makes it float?

**3** Cut the hairs off one of the dandelion seeds and blow on it. Measure how far it goes.

What happens if you wet a dandelion seed?

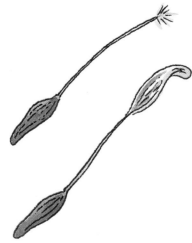

What would be the best weather for a dandelion plant to scatter its seeds?

# ANIMAL TRANSPORT

Some fruits and seeds have hooks on them. They stick to the fur or feathers of animals and birds. They also stick to people's clothes.

If you have a dog or cat, comb it after it has been for a walk. Can you find any of these fruits and seeds?

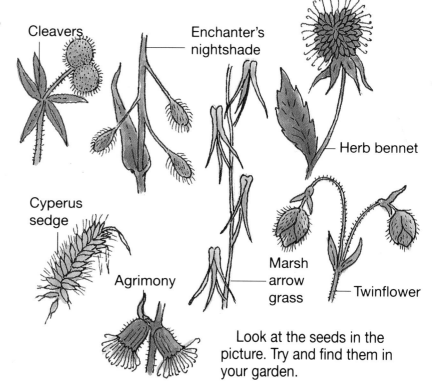

Cleavers

Enchanter's nightshade

Herb bennet

Cyperus sedge

Agrimony

Marsh arrow grass

Twinflower

Look at the seeds in the picture. Try and find them in your garden.

Seeds are also scattered in the mud on animals' feet and on people's boots and shoes. Put your boots on and go for a walk along a muddy path.

**1** Scrape the mud from your boots when you get home.

**2** Fill a flower pot with potting soil. Sprinkle the mud over the surface and water it.

Do any seeds grow? What do they turn into? Why do you think you have to use potting soil and not ordinary soil for this experiment?

## Fruit and Nuts

Many seeds are surrounded by a fleshy fruit. These fruits are eaten by birds. The seeds pass through their bodies and grow in a new place. Squirrels hide nuts and forget where they are hidden. These often grow into new plants.

# LOOKING AT LEAVES

**Nearly all plants have leaves. Leaves come in all shapes and sizes. Mostly they are green in color. A few leaves are other colors such as red or orange, but they still have green color or *pigment* inside. Leaves use this pigment and sunlight to make food for the plant.**

Some leaves are needle shaped and come from trees called conifers. Other leaves are flat and come from broad-leaved trees such as the oak.

These are tree leaves but all other plants have leaves too.

Collect as many different kinds of leaves as you can find.

**1** Spread the leaves out on some sheets of newspaper. Cover them with some more newspapers.

**2** Weigh them down with heavy books.

**3** After a few days your leaves will be dry and flat. You can then stick them in a book or on a wallchart.

**4** Label each leaf, saying what kind of plant it came from. Say where and when you collected it.

# LEAF PRINTS

You can make spatter leaf prints with some more leaves.

**You will need:** leaves; white paper; paint; old toothbrush; newspaper; ruler.

**1** Lay plenty of newspaper on the table and put a sheet of white paper on it. Carefully arrange a large leaf on the sheet of paper.

**2** Mix some paint so that it is quite runny and dip an old toothbrush in it.

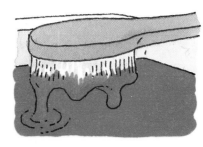

**3** Hold the brush just above the paper with the leaf on it. Run the ruler through the bristles of the brush.

**4** Paint will flick down on to the paper and leaf. Keep doing this until all the white paper is covered.

**5** When the paint is dry, carefully lift the leaf.

## Plants and Light

We have seen what happens when alfalfa seeds are kept in the dark. Here are two more experiments to find out what light does to plants.

**1** Water a potted plant and cover it with a cardboard box.

**2** Cut a small hole in one side of the box.

Keep the plant covered for a few days. What happens to the plant? Why is this?

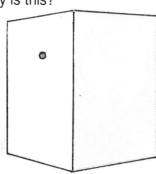

**1** Cut one of your initials out of a peel-off sticker. Stick it on a plant leaf or on an apple still growing on the tree.

**2** Leave your initial there for a week or two. Then carefully peel it off. What do you notice?

# THIRSTY PLANTS

All animals including humans and birds drink water. We could go several weeks without food, but without water we would die in three or four days. Some animals live in water. So do some plants. But do plants drink water, and if so what do they do with it?

## DISAPPEARING WATER

**You will need:** a weed; jar; poster board; water; oil; tape.

**1** Dig up a garden weed and wash the roots clean. Half fill a jar with water and stand the plant in it.

**2** Cut a slit and a hole in the poster board. Tape it to the top of the jar.

**3** Lift one corner of the poster board. Pour a little oil down the inside of the jar so that it forms a layer on the surface.

**4** Set up another jar with water, oil, and poster board but no plant. What happens to the water level? Why was oil put on the water?

### Going up

How does water get up to the leaves of a plant?

**1** Half fill a jar with water and put a few drops of red food coloring or ink in it. Stand a freshly cut stick of celery in the jar.

**2** After a few days, cut across the stem. Look at it with a magnifying glass. What has happened to it?

# RAINBOW FLOWERS

If you can get a white carnation flower, split part of its stem lengthwise. Put one half into a jar of water colored red. Put the other half into a jar of water colored blue. What happens to the flower? Can you make a flower which has three different colors?

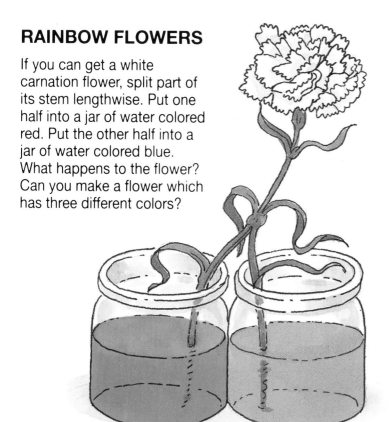

## Do Plants Give Off Water?

Find a small plastic bag which has no holes in it. Tie the bag over a leafy shoot on a potted plant. Or tie the bag over a leafy twig on a tree in the garden.

Look at the bag the next day. What is inside it? Where has it come from?

## MAKE A MINIATURE GARDEN

You can learn a lot about plants by making a miniature garden. *Mosses, liverworts,* and *ferns* are good plants to choose because they like damp places.

**1** Search around the garden or some vacant lots for tufts of mosses, liverworts, or small ferns. Dig some of these up carefully and put them in a plastic bag.

**2** Put some damp potting soil in the bottom of the jar.

**3** Gently push the plants into position with a thin stick. Put the stopper on the jar and rest it on a windowsill.

**You will need:** a large stoppered jar; potting soil; plants; thin stick.

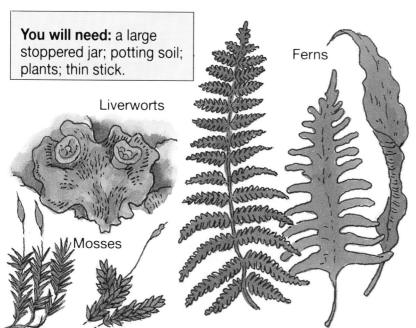

Liverworts

Mosses

Ferns

Where do the plants get their water from? Why do the plants not need feeding? Why could you not keep small animals like this?

# LARGE AND SMALL

**There are millions of animals in the world. Some are large, some are small. Here are some pictures of animals. How many do you know?**

Scientists divide animals up into two groups. One large group of animals has a backbone and bony *skeleton* inside their bodies. These are called *vertebrates.* All the other animals which do not have a backbone are called *invertebrates.*

Most invertebrates are quite small and, although they do not have bones, some do have a hard skin or shell around the outside to protect them. Crabs, lobsters, and beetles are examples.

Look again at the picture. Which are vertebrates and which are invertebrates?

18

# PITFALL TRAPS

Many small animals only come out at night. You can see what small animals live in your garden if you make a pitfall trap.

**You will need:** a plastic bottle; piece of wood; 2 stones.

**1** Ask an adult to cut the neck off a plastic bottle.

**2** Dig a hole and sink the bottom half of the bottle into the ground.

**3** Place two stones on opposite sides of the container. Put the piece of wood over the top to keep out the rain.

**4** Your trap is now ready to use. Any small animals that run across the ground at night will fall into your trap and be unable to get out.

Look at your trap at least twice every day.

ALWAYS set small animals free.

## Trapped!

Set pitfall traps near large plants and under hedges and trees. You might catch these animals shown below.

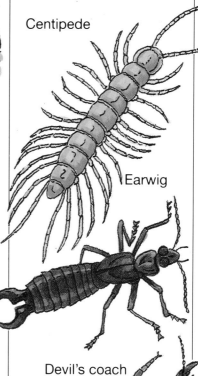

Centipede

Earwig

Devil's coach horse

**1** Put breadcrumbs and meat as *bait* in the traps. Do you catch different animals if the trap contains different bait?

**2** Take the traps away afterward as animals could fall in and die.

# ANIMAL HOMES

**Every animal must have three things to survive. It needs food, shelter, and a place to rear its young. Different animals live in different kinds of shelter. Why is this? You can find out in these next experiments.**

## DOWN UNDER

Farmers are lucky that earthworms make their homes in the soil. You can see why if you set up a worm farm.

**You will need:** a large plastic jar; sand; soil; 3 dead leaves; black paper; rubber bands; earthworms.

**1** Fill up your jar with layers of moist sand and soil. Put the dead leaves on top.

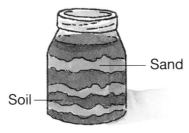

Sand

Soil

**2** Put two earthworms in the jar. Cover the top with black paper and make a few air-holes.

**3** Wrap black paper around the jar, and fix it with the rubber bands.

Keep it somewhere cool for a week. Then take off the covering. What can you see?

Use different kinds of raw vegetables and leaves. Which foods do earthworms prefer?

# WET OR DRY? DARK OR LIGHT?

**You will need:** a shallow plastic box (with a lid); black paper; plastic wrap; cotton; pencil; 10 sow bugs.

**1** Draw a line across the middle of the tray. Make some small air-holes in the lid.

**2** Wet a tuft of cotton and put it at one end of the tray. Put a tuft of dry cotton at the other end.

Wet

Dry

**3** Place the 10 sow bugs in the center of the tray and put the lid on.

After 10 minutes remove the lid. Count how many sow bugs are in each half of the tray.

**4** Remove the cotton and cover half of the tray with plastic wrap. Cover the other half with black paper.

Put your sow bugs in the middle of the tray again.

**5** After 10 minutes check the sow bugs. Which do sow bugs like best, a wet, dry, light, or dark place?

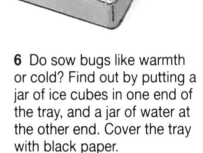

**6** Do sow bugs like warmth or cold? Find out by putting a jar of ice cubes in one end of the tray, and a jar of water at the other end. Cover the tray with black paper.

**7** After 10 minutes check the sow bugs. Which do they like best, cold or warm places?

Try this experiment with other small animals such as small slugs, snails, and earthworms. Do they all like the same things?

# WATCHING INSECTS

*Insects* are invertebrates. All insects have six legs. Their bodies are divided up into three parts. They have tough skin around their bodies to protect them. Most insects have four wings, although some have only two wings and some none at all.

## KEEPING STICK INSECTS

Male stick insects are very rare. Most stick insects are females which lay the eggs.

**You will need:** a large plastic jar or an old fish tank (to make a cage); small bottle of water; old pair of pantyhose; stems with leaves; cotton; stick insects.

Stick insects feed mainly on privet leaves. They will also eat the leaves of ivy, holly, and primrose plants.

**1** Put the stems in the water.

**2** Wrap cotton around the top of the bottle to keep the stick insects from falling in.

**3** Place three stick insects in the cage and cover it with a piece of the pantyhose.

Always keep the food fresh, and the cage clean.

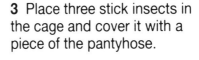

**4** If any *eggs* are laid, keep them in a small jar lid until they hatch. Keep the babies in a separate, small jar and feed them on young leaves.

**5** Use a ruler to measure how much one of your stick insects grows. How do stick insects make themselves look like sticks? How does this help them?

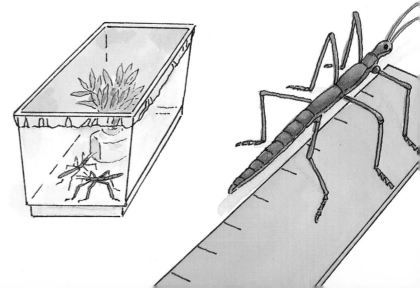

# BREEDING FLIES

**You will need:** a plastic bottle; raw meat; old pair of pantyhose; black paper; tape.

ALWAYS wash your hands after touching flies.

**1** Ask an adult to cut the top off a plastic bottle to make a funnel.

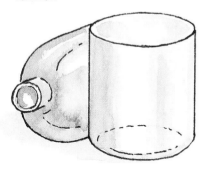

**2** Put two or three small pieces of raw meat into the bottom of the bottle.

**3** Fix your funnel with tape to the top of the bottle. You now have a fly trap to put outside.

Leave any trapped flies for a few hours. Then free them. You should now be able to see white fly eggs on the meat.

**4** Cover the top of the trap with a piece of the pantyhose and wrap the black paper around the sides. Put the trap in a warm place.

**5** Look at the eggs every day. Before long they will hatch into *maggots*, then brown *pupae*, and finally adult flies. Make a chart to record how long each stage takes.

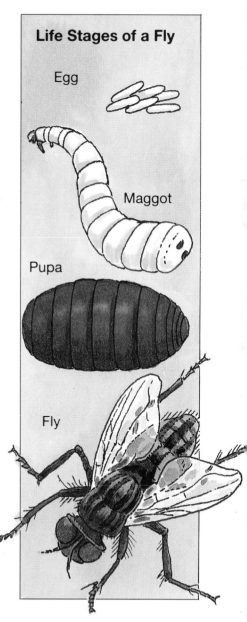

## Life Stages of a Fly

Egg

Maggot

Pupa

Fly

Butterflies and moths also go through four stages. Do you know what they are? You can try to find out.

# SLUGS AND SNAILS

**Slugs and snails are small invertebrate animals. They belong to a big group of animals called *mollusks*. Slugs and many snails live on land. Some other snails live in ponds, lakes, and rivers. Cockles, mussels, cuttlefish, squid, and octopuses are mollusks that live in the sea.**

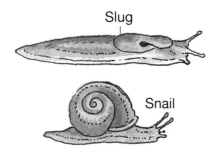

Slug

Snail

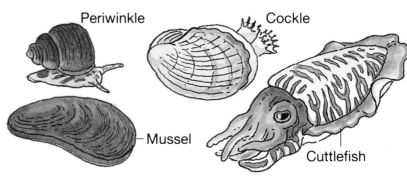

Periwinkle

Cockle

Mussel

Cuttlefish

## HOME FROM HOME

Slugs and snails are easy to keep for a week or two.

**You will need:** a large clear plastic jar; damp soil; stone or piece of bark; slugs or snails.

**1** Put the soil in the bottom of the jar and lay your stone or the piece of bark on the top.

**2** Put your slugs or snails in their cage. Feed them with lettuce, cabbage, or stinging nettle leaves on different days.

Always remove any stale food. Which foods do slugs and snails like best?

**3** Slugs and snails lay small white eggs in the soil. If you can find any, pick them up with a spoon. Look at them with a magnifying glass.

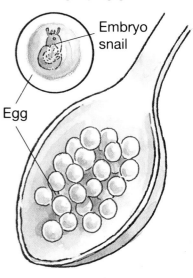

Embryo snail

Egg

Can you see the baby animals growing inside the eggs? How long do they take to hatch?

24

### Slimy Trails

What helps slugs or snails to move?

**1** Place a slug or a snail on a piece of black paper, and watch it creep across. Can you see the trail of slime it leaves? This slime helps the slug or snail to move easily.

**2** Let a slug or snail crawl up the inside of a clean plastic jar. Look at the animal with a magnifying glass. Can you see its muscles moving? Can you see the slug or snail's breathing hole? How many times does it open and close in two minutes?

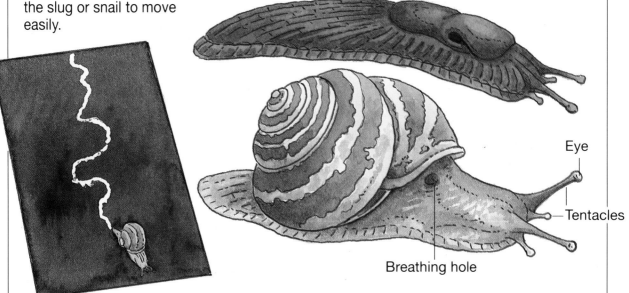

Eye

Tentacles

Breathing hole

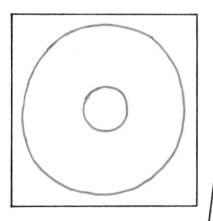

## SLUG AND SNAIL RACES

**1** Find a large sheet of paper and draw a big circle on it. In the middle of this large circle draw a small circle.

**2** Put two slugs in the center circle. Time how long it takes for the fastest one to cross the outer circle.

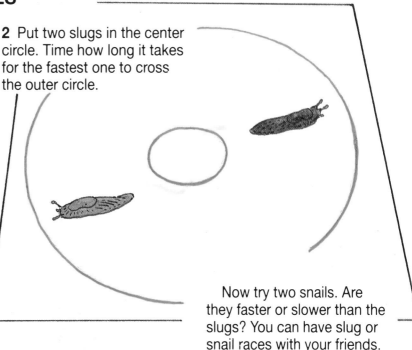

Now try two snails. Are they faster or slower than the slugs? You can have slug or snail races with your friends.

25

# FOOD CHAINS

**Many animals feed on plants. They are called *herbivores*. Some animals feed on other animals. We say they are *carnivores*.**

The animals that carnivores eat either feed on other, smaller carnivores or they feed on herbivores. In a way animals and plants are linked together by their food in what is called a *food chain.* This is a food chain:

Cabbage plant   ⟶   Slug   ⟶   Thrush   ⟶   Cat

## A SIMPLE FOOD CHAIN

Green aphids and black aphids are very small insects. They feed on many garden plants, sucking the plant juices.

In late spring or summer look for aphids on the shoots of rose bushes. Look at them with a magnifying glass.

Can you see how the aphids feed? Aphids do not lay eggs for most of the summer. Instead they produce live young.

Ladybugs are carnivores as they eat aphids. You can see this for yourself.

> **You will need:** aphids; ladybugs; bottle of water; large jar; old pair of pantyhose; cotton; rubber band.

**1** Find a rose shoot with aphids on it.

**2** Put it in a small bottle of water and wrap cotton around the top of the bottle to stop the aphids falling in.

**3** Put the bottle, rose shoot, and aphids in a large jar. Gently place two or three ladybugs on the rose shoot.

**4** Cover the jar with a piece of pantyhose.

**5** Watch with a magnifying glass. How does a ladybug catch and eat aphids? What does it do with the leftovers? Draw a food chain to sum up what happens.

# KEEPING SPIDERS

Spiders are small carnivores. You will find them outside in corners and cracks of walls, under bark and in large clumps of plants. There are also several kinds of spiders living in houses. Look at your spiders carefully. How many legs do they have? How many parts are there to their bodies? Are spiders insects?

**You will need:** a large jar or clear plastic box; damp soil; pair of old pantyhose; roll of paper; rubber band; spider.

**1** Put a layer of damp soil in the bottom of the container, and the roll of paper for the spider to hide in.

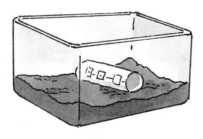

**2** Cover the container with a piece of the pantyhose. Keep it in place with the rubber band.

Feed the spider on flies or other small insects, and a little water in a tin lid.

If you want your spider to spin a web it must have a bigger home. A small fish tank is ideal with a branched twig on which to make its web.

Draw the different stages in web-building.

What happens if you touch the finished web with a blade of grass? Make a small hole in the web, does the spider mend it? Look at the web with a magnifying glass. What makes the web sticky? What is the web used for?

## Who Eats What?

In the picture you can see herbivores and carnivores. You can use them to draw your own food chains.

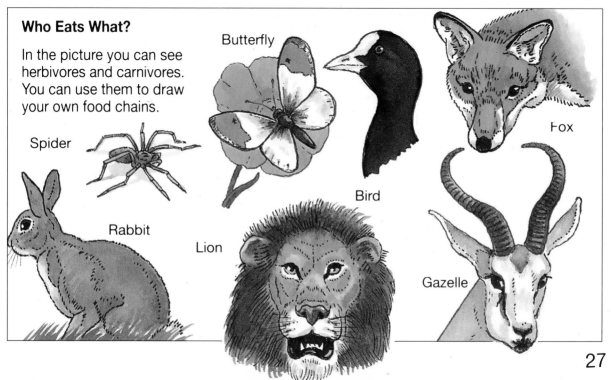

Butterfly

Spider

Bird

Fox

Rabbit

Lion

Gazelle

# DINING OUT

Some of the most common vertebrate animals are birds. Birds are everywhere. There are birds in the country, towns, and cities, by the sea and high in the mountains. Many birds would die in winter when insects and plant foods are difficult to find, if people did not give them food. A bird table and bird pudding are useful things to make.

Quail

House sparrow

Gull

Golden eagle

## A FRUITY TREAT

Here is a special treat you can make for the birds.

**You will need:** a large yogurt container; mixing bowl; spoon; cup full of a mixture of seeds, raisins, currants, nuts, cake crumbs; scraps of cheese; cup of fat.

**1** Put your mixture into the mixing bowl.

**2** Ask an adult to melt the fat and stir it into the mixture. Let the mixture set.

ALWAYS ask an adult to help you heat things.

**3** Turn it out on a bird table and watch all the birds enjoying it.

# MAKE A BIRD TABLE

**You will need:** a wooden board (20 in x 12 in; 50 cm x 30 cm); 4 strips of wood (¹/2 in; 1.5 cm wide); stake (60 in; 1.5 m long); large plastic flower pot; hammer; nails.

**1** Nail the strips of wood around the board. Leave gaps at the corners so that the table can be easily swept clean and the rain water can run away.

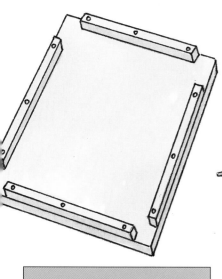

ALWAYS ask an adult to help you saw and nail wood.

**2** Nail the plastic pot upside down on the stake and nail the board – your table top – to the stake.

**3** Dig a hole and firmly fix the stake in the ground.

Choose a spot where you can see easily, but do not put the bird table too near trees and bushes where cats and gray squirrels can hide. The flower pot is to help stop these animals from climbing up onto your table.

**4** Ask an adult to paint the top of your bird table with waterproof paint or varnish before you use it.

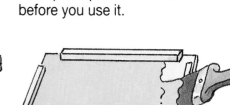

Only feed the birds during the winter months when food is scarce. They will enjoy bread, unsalted nuts, bacon rind, cooked potato, and other table scraps.

NEVER feed birds salted food.

# NEIGHBORHOOD BIRDS

**One way to tell what birds usually eat is to look at their beaks. Look at the pictures. How are the beaks different? Where do all these birds find their food?**

When birds come to your bird table, look carefully at their beaks.

Swan

Owl

Finch

Seed-eaters such as sparrows and finches have a shorter, blunter beak.

Duck

Falcon

Swallow

Ducks, geese, and swans have flattened beaks for sieving food from water.

Flesh-eating birds, such as hawks, owls, and eagles have hooked beaks.

Birds like swallows and robins, which eat insects, have a narrow pointed beak.

## SPLASHING AROUND

If you feed the birds in winter you may save their lives. But birds also need to drink and bathe all year long. So give them clean water daily.

**1** Dig a hole and sink your container in the ground. Just cover the bottom with water. Make sure it is not too close to any buildings.

Some birds like to dry-clean themselves. They bathe in dust.

**2** Fill a shallow box with dry sieved soil. Put it in a quiet place. You could mix a little sand with the soil if it is to go on the lawn. What birds come to bathe in it?

**You will need:** a tray or garbage can lid; water.

# BIRD FEEDERS

If you don't have room for a bird table, don't worry. There are other bird feeders to make which will attract birds near your home.

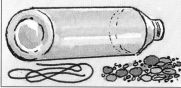

**You will need:** a clean plastic bottle; string; bird food.

**1** Cut the top off your bottle. Make a hole on each side of the bottom half.

**2** Thread one end of the string through one of the holes and knot it.

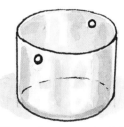

**3** Loop the string over and thread the other end through the second hole. Knot it. Now you have a handle to hang your feeder up on a branch. Fill it with unsalted peanuts, bread or cake crumbs.

Even bottle tops can be filled with food for the birds. Nail them onto a piece of wood and fill them with fat or some of the bird pudding you made on page 28.

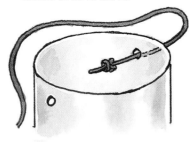

Watch the birds carefully that visit your feeders. Look at the way they cling to the food. Do they peck little bits of food or do they take large lumps and fly away with them to a safe place?

Do the same birds come back every day? Ask an adult to help you name them.

Keep a bird feeder chart like this:

| Date | Time of day | Weather | Name of bird | What the bird did | What the bird ate | Was the bird alone? |
|------|-------------|---------|--------------|-------------------|-------------------|---------------------|
|      |             |         |              |                   |                   |                     |

# HELPING OUR WILDLIFE

**There are many kinds of plants and animals in the world. But lots have died out, or become *extinct*, and many more kinds are in danger. This is mainly because the places where they live are being destroyed.**

If you enjoy looking at plants and animals, you will want to help them live happily near your home. You can do this by providing homes, food and water for them. You can do some of these things even if you do not have a garden.

## NEST BOXES

Birds use nest boxes not only to rear their young in the spring and summer, but also to sleep in during the winter.

> **You will need:** a plank of wood 6 in (15 cm) wide and 5 ft (150 cm) long; strip of rubber; nails; hammer; drill; fastener.

**1** Saw the plank into the six pieces shown. Care is needed with this as you have to cut the wood at an angle.

You must also angle the cut between the front and the roof to give sloping edges. Look at the picture.

> ALWAYS ask an adult to help you saw and drill wood.

**2** Drill a hole (about 1 in; (3 cm) across) near the top of the front section. Drill a few small drainage holes in the floor.

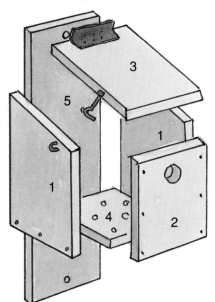

**3** Nail the strip of rubber to the lid as a hinge. Then nail the remaining pieces together.

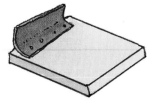

**4** Fix the catch to the side.

Put up your box well before the nesting season. In the fall or winter is a good time. Fix it to a tree trunk, wall, or fence where it is out of reach of cats. See that the box is not in full sunlight.

Cut at an angle here

| 8 in  1 | 10 in  1 | 2 | 3 | 4 | 5 |
|---------|----------|---|---|---|---|
| side | side | front | roof | base | back |
| 10 in | 8 in | 8 in | 8½ in | 4 in | 18 in |

# MAKE A WILDLIFE GARDEN

If you can find a spare corner of the garden, make your own nature reserve. You can either grow the plants you need from seeds or ask an adult for cuttings. Weed plants you can find in the country.

**1** Dig up a small clump of stinging nettles and plant them in your garden. These will provide food for the *caterpillars* of butterflies.

ALWAYS wear an old pair of thick gloves when handling nettles and thistles.

You could also plant Michaelmas daisies and wild strawberry.

Wild strawberry

Michaelmas daisies

**2** Find an old rotting log, put it on the ground and sprinkle dead tree leaves around it. It will make a home for many small invertebrates.

If you have enough space, then make nesting boxes for birds and don't forget your bird table, bird feeders, and bird bath.

Make your garden a place where wildlife will want to live. Then you will be doing your bit to save our wildlife.

Mahogany tree

Rafflesia

Scarlet macaw

Tiger

There are many animals and plants in the world that are *endangered*. Look at the picture. Why are these living things threatened? Is there anything we can do to help save them?

# GLOSSARY

**Here are the meanings of some words you might have met for the first time in this book.**

**BAIT:** food used to attract and catch animals, birds, and fish.

**BULBS:** the swollen underground parts (leaves and buds) of certain plants.

**CARNIVORES:** animals that eat flesh or meat.

**CARPEL:** the part of a flower that makes the seeds.

**CATERPILLARS:** the feeding and growing stages of butterflies or moths, which hatch from the eggs.

**CUTTINGS:** pieces cut off a plant and set in soil or water to grow.

**EGGS:** the round or oval objects laid by many female animals in which young animals begin life.

**EMBRYO:** a tiny plant that is still inside the seed; a young animal before it is born or a bird before it is hatched.

**ENDANGERED:** any species of plants or animals whose numbers are growing so small that they are in danger of dying out completely.

**EXTINCT:** no longer to be found in the world.

**FERNS:** kinds of plants, often with feathery leaves, which do not produce seeds. Instead the new plants come from spores.

**FOOD CHAIN:** a series of living things that depend on each other for food.

**HERBIVORES:** plant-eating animals.

**INSECTS:** small six-legged animals with no backbones.

**INVERTEBRATES:** animals that do not have a backbone.

**LIFE CYCLE:** the changes through which an animal or plant passes as it grows to be an adult.

**LIVERWORTS:** low, green, mosslike plants which live in shady, moist places.

**MAGGOTS:** the feeding and growing stages of some kinds of fly.

**MOLLUSKS:** small animals with a soft body and usually one or two hard shells, such as snails, oysters, and cockles. Most mollusks have thin fingerlike sensitive parts called tentacles.

**MOSSES:** small green, tufted, low-growing plants that usually grow in damp places.

**PIGMENT:** any substance in the cells of animals and plants that gives them color.

**POLLEN:** a yellow powder made by flowers.

**PUPAE:** the resting stages of certain insects, such as flies, butterflies, and moths, which come before the adults.

**SEPAL:** one of the green, leaflike parts which protect a flower when it is in bud.

**SKELETON:** the framework of bones inside people and some other animals.

**STAMEN:** one of the parts of a flower which makes the yellow powder pollen.

**VERTEBRATES:** animals with a backbone.

**WEEDS:** wild plants growing where they are not wanted.